50 MONTH-BY-MONTH Draw & Write Prompts

by Danielle Blood

SCHOLASTIC
PROFESSIONAL BOOKS

NEW YORK • TORONTO • LONDON • AUCKLAND • SYDNEY
MEXICO CITY • NEW DELHI • HONG KONG • BUENOS AIRES

For Lexie, Jamie, Allegra, and Ryan

Cover design by Maria Lilja
Interior design by Solutions by Design, Inc.
Cover and interior illustrations by James Graham Hale

ISBN: 0-439-27176-2

2 3 4 5 6 7 8 9 10   40   08 07 06 05 04 03 02

Contents

Introduction

Welcome to *50 Month-by-Month Draw & Write Prompts*, a fun-filled way to motivate emergent writers to put their ideas into words! These ready-to-go activity pages invite children to draw a picture and then write about what they've drawn. The topics tie in to your favorite themes throughout the year: harvest, animals, 100th day of school, holidays, weather, classroom community, and much more! The variety of fun formats helps keep students' interest and motivation high.

Each reproducible page includes easy-to-read directions and prompts for both drawing and writing. Drawing a picture as a pre-writing activity encourages children to think about the topic and express themselves in a way that is comfortable and fun for them. Once they've drawn the picture, they are ready to write. Short writing prompts then invite children to use details from their picture to generate ideas for writing. Many pages include word banks for additional guidance.

By sparking their interest in a topic and providing the scaffolding that emergent writers need, *50 Month-by-Month Draw & Write Prompts* helps children build fluency and confidence as writers. Children will enjoy sharing their artwork and writing with teachers, classmates, and family members. Happy drawing and writing!

How to Use This Book

The draw and write prompts in this book are organized by month to take you through the school year and summer. The Table of Contents lists each prompt by title, month, and theme to make it easy to tie the activities in to your curriculum. The activity pages are designed to be flexible and easy to use; you can use them in any order you wish or in the order in which they are presented here. It's a good idea to present a draw and write prompt after you've discussed its topic with your class. The more students know about a topic, the more information they'll have to write about it.

Pre-Writing

To begin, choose the prompt that you wish to use and make a photocopy of the reproducible page for each student. Distribute pencils and crayons or markers. Read the drawing prompt aloud and show students the drawing space on the page. As children draw, encourage them to add details to their pictures that they can incorporate into their writing later. Once they've finished drawing, invite children to share their pictures with a partner or with the whole class. Talking about their pictures is another helpful pre-writing activity.

Writing

Next, read aloud the writing prompts. If children need additional guidance, brainstorm responses and write them on the board or on chart paper. When children are ready to write on their own, encourage them to use their drawings to generate ideas and details for their writing. If the page includes a word bank, explain that children can refer to it for ideas or for help with spelling.

Sharing

Invite children to share their writing with you, or with a partner, a small group, or the whole class. Display the completed draw and write prompts on a bulletin board or compile them to create a collaborative class book. Then encourage children to take home their prompts to share with their families. You might also compile each child's prompts for a particular month, staple them together with a cover, and send them home as a book.

Formats

The diverse formats included in this book keeps children's interest high and helps them produce varied types of writing. It also provides them with practice in following different kinds of directions. The activity pages for the beginning of the school year invite children to draw a picture and then follow prompts to write about it. Word banks are provided for extra support. As the draw and write prompts move through the year, the following formats are introduced:

- **Interviews:** Children draw a picture of an interview and write questions and answers.

- **Sequencing:** Children draw and write about a sequence of steps.

- **How to Draw...:** Children follow easy steps to draw a picture and then complete the prompts to write a short fictional story.

- **Charts:** Children fill in a chart with pictures and writing.

- **Connect the Dots:** Children connect the dots to complete a picture and follow prompts to write about it.

- **Color by Number:** On the first page, children color a picture by number to reveal a surprise. On the second page, children draw their own picture and write about it.

A Summer Memory

by _____

A memory is something you remember. Think of something special that you did over the summer. In the box, draw a picture of your memory.

Word Bank

- swimming
- riding
- playing
- bicycle
- camp
- family
- vacation
- beach
- mountains
- visit
- fun
- happy
- proud
- excited

In this picture, I am _____

_____

This was special because _____

_____

When I was doing this, I felt _____

_____

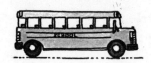

The First Day of School

by _____

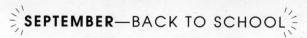

✏️ **In the box, draw a picture of yourself on the first day of school.**

Word Bank

excited

nervous

happy

kindergarten

first

second

classroom

friend

classmates

teacher

On the first day of school, I felt _____

When I got to school, I saw _____

My teacher's name is _____

This is the grade I am now in: _____

The best thing that happened on the first day of school was _____

_____

All About Me

by _____

 In the mirror, draw a picture of yourself.

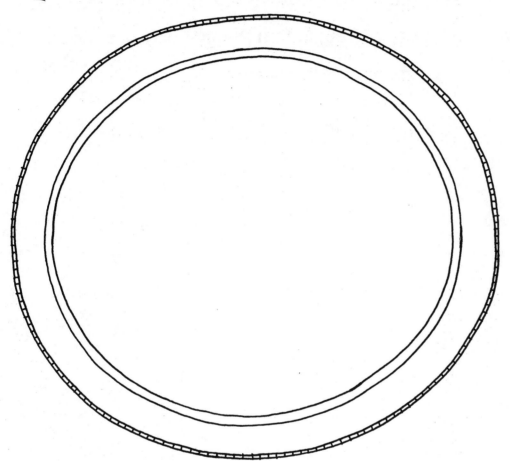

Word Bank

draw
swim
play
write
read
build
blocks
nice
friendly
funny
shy
generous
helpful

Hello! My name is _____

I am _____

I can _____

I like to _____

The following words describe me: _____

_____

My Goals

by _____

 **Draw a picture of something you would like to learn how to do this year.**

Word Bank

read

write

learn

play

ride

add

subtract

bicycle

teacher

sister

brother

friend

parent

I would like to learn how to _____

_____

I would like to learn this because _____

_____

Someone who could help me learn this is _____

Our Classroom

by _____

 Draw a picture of your favorite part of your classroom.

Word Bank

center

art

blocks

writing

library

books

pencils

paint

draw

build

read

fun

This is a picture of _____

In this area, there are _____

_____

In this area, I can _____

_____

I like this area because _____

_____

New Friends Interview

by _____

Draw a picture of yourself interviewing a classmate at school.

Then think of two questions to ask your classmate. In the boxes on the left, write the questions. Then ask a classmate the questions. In the boxes on the right, write his or her answers.

QUESTIONS	ANSWERS
1. _____ _____ _____	1. _____ _____ _____
2. _____ _____ _____	2. _____ _____ _____

50 Month-by-Month Draw & Write Prompts Scholastic Professional Books

Happy Birthday, Johnny Appleseed!

Imagine that you are going to throw a birthday party for Johnny Appleseed. Draw a picture of the party below.

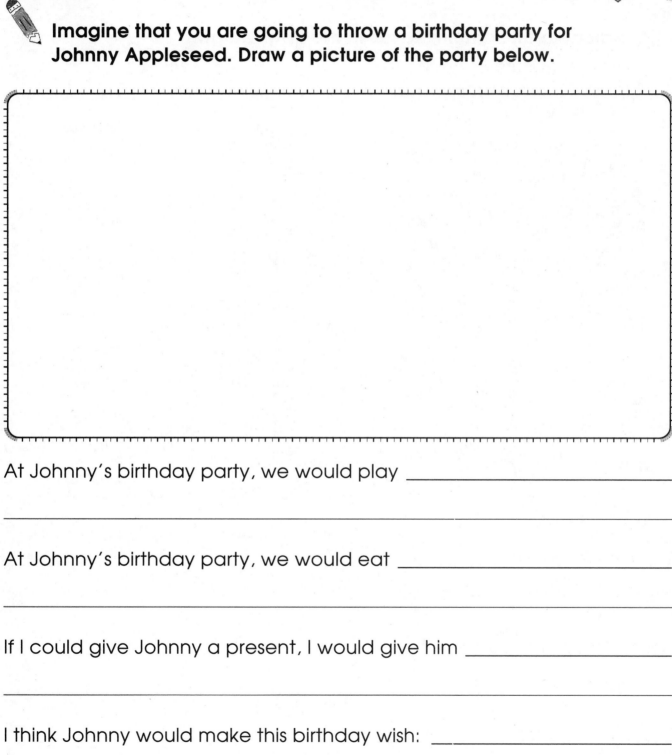

At Johnny's birthday party, we would play _____

_____

At Johnny's birthday party, we would eat _____

_____

If I could give Johnny a present, I would give him _____

_____

I think Johnny would make this birthday wish: _____

_____

Autumn Leaves

by _____

 Add colorful autumn leaves to the trees below.

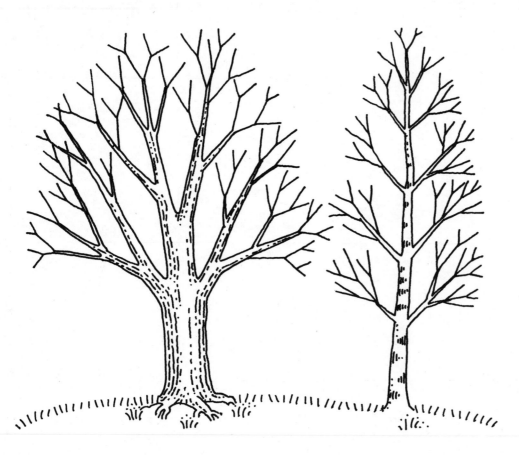

Word Bank

leaves
trees
autumn
red
yellow
orange
brown
pile
rake
jump
play
crunch

This is a picture of _____

_____

The colors of the leaves are _____

_____

When the leaves fall, I like to _____

_____

50 Month-by-Month Draw & Write Prompts Scholastic Professional Books

Firefighters Help Us

by _____

✏️ **Draw a picture of a firefighter.**

Word Bank

- firefighter
- fire truck
- hose
- hat
- dog
- red
- shiny
- siren
- rescue
- save
- help
- people
- building

This picture shows _____

_____

The firefighter in this picture is _____

_____

Firefighters are important because they _____

_____

My Jack-o'-Lantern

by _____

How do you draw a jack-o'-lantern? In the boxes, draw each step. Then write about the steps.

1. First, I _____
_____

2. Then, I _____
_____

3. Next, I _____
_____

4. Last, I _____
_____

My Halloween Costume

by _____

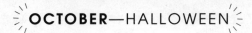

Draw a picture of yourself in your Halloween costume.

Word Bank

clown

witch

wizard

superhero

princess

cat

makeup

hat

cape

scary

pretty

funny

cute

In this picture, I am dressed as _____

For my costume, I put on _____

I looked _____

Next year I would like to dress as _____

Book Week Bookmark

by _____

 On the bookmark, draw a picture of yourself reading your favorite book. Then cut out your bookmark.

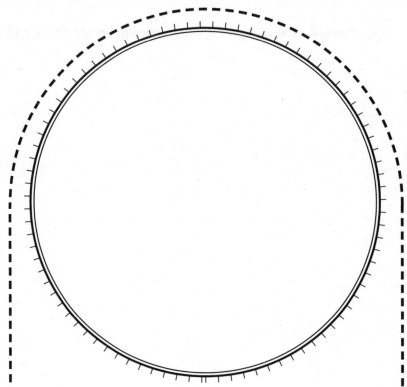

In this picture, the book I am reading is

_____

_____

This book is about _____

_____

I like this book because _____

_____

_____

Harvest Time

by _____

Imagine that you are a farmer and it is harvest time. What did you grow? In the box, draw a picture of yourself with your crops.

Word Bank

vegetables

fruit

grain

apples

pumpkins

squash

carrots

corn

pick

tools

red

orange

green

yellow

In this picture, I am _____

_____

This is what I grew: _____

_____

The colors of my harvest are _____

_____

If I Were a Pilgrim...

by _____

Imagine that you are a Pilgrim.
Then draw a picture of yourself as a Pilgrim.

If I were a Pilgrim, I would wear _____

_____

I would live in _____

I would like to _____

My life would be different than it is today because _____

_____

50 Month-by-Month Draw & Write Prompts Scholastic Professional Books

Giving Thanks

by ______________________________

Draw a picture of something you're thankful for.

This is a picture of ______________________________

____

I am thankful for this because ______________________________

____

I am also thankful for ______________________________

____

How to Draw a Turkey

by _____

 **Follow these steps to draw a turkey.
On the next page, draw a turkey.**

Step 1

Step 2

Step 3

Step 4

Step 5

Step 6

Draw & Write About a Turkey

by _____

✏️ **In the box, draw a turkey.**

[drawing box]

Once there was a turkey named _____

He was _____

He was unlike other turkeys because he could _____

_____

He could also _____

_____

How to Draw the Mayflower

by _____

**Follow these steps to draw the Mayflower.
On the next page, draw the Mayflower.**

Step 1

Step 2

Step 3

Step 4

Step 5

Step 6

Draw & Write About the Mayflower

by _____

 In the box, draw the Mayflower.

In 1620, the Mayflower sailed from England to _____

_____

In this picture, there are _____

_____

The Pilgrims aboard the Mayflower wanted to _____

_____

Favorite Wintertime Activities

by _____

In each box, draw a picture of something you like to do during the winter. Write the name of the activity below each drawing. Then fill in the chart.

Draw your winter activity picture here.	I like doing this because...	My favorite thing about this is...
Name of Activity _____		
Name of Activity _____		

Bundle Up!

by _____

 How do you dress before going outside in the cold? In the boxes, draw each step. Then write about the steps.

1. First, I _____

_____

2. Then, I _____

_____

3. Next, I _____

_____

4. Last, I _____

_____

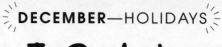

How I Celebrate...

by _____

Draw a picture of yourself celebrating your winter holiday.

The winter holiday I celebrate is _____

In this picture, I am _____

_____

I celebrate this holiday with _____

_____

My favorite part of this holiday is _____

_____

A Sleepy Surprise

by _____

Connect the dots from 1 to 42. Then fill in the blanks below.

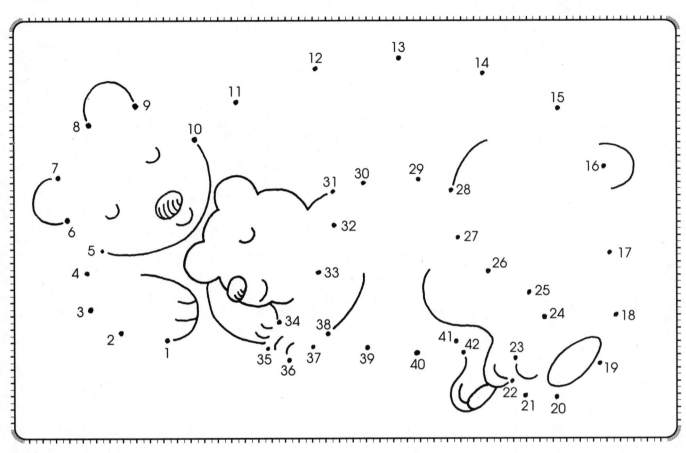

In this picture, _____

_____

They are sleeping because _____

_____

They will wake up when it is _____

I imagine that they are dreaming about _____

_____

My New Year's Wish

by _____

What is something that you wish will happen in the new year? Draw a picture of it.

My wish is _____

_____

I hope my wish comes true, because _____

_____

If my wish came true, I would feel _____

_____

50 Month-by-Month Draw & Write Prompts Scholastic Professional Books

Martin Luther King, Jr.'s Dream

by _____

Martin Luther King, Jr.'s dream was that _____

_____

Do you have a dream? Draw a picture of it in the box.

[drawing box]

My dream is _____

_____

In my dream, people would _____

_____

Here is something I can do to make my dream come true: _____

_____

How to Draw a Penguin

Name _____

 **Follow these steps to draw a penguin.
On the next page, draw a penguin.**

Step 1	Step 2
Step 3	Step 4
Step 5	Step 6

50 Month-by-Month Draw & Write Prompts Scholastic Professional Books

Draw & Write About a Penguin

by _____

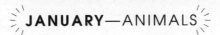

✏️ **In the box, draw a penguin.**

[drawing box]

Hello! My name is _____

I live in _____

I like to _____

I can also _____

I wish I could _____

_____

When It's Cold Outside...

by _____

Draw a picture of a wintertime scene. In the picture, include yourself, other people, and animals.

This picture shows _____

_____

When it's cold outside, some people like to _____

_____

When it's cold outside, people wear _____

_____

Presidents' Day Interview

by _____

Imagine that you are going to interview the president. In the box, draw a picture of yourself interviewing the president.

Think about what you would ask the president.
Then imagine how the president might answer.
The first question has been provided for you.

Interviewer: What do you like about being president?

President: _____

_____

Interviewer: _____

_____

President: _____

_____

Happy Valentine's Day!

by _____

 In the heart, draw a picture of someone you would like to wish a Happy Valentine's Day to. Then write that person a message.

TO:

_____

Roses are _____.

Violets are blue.

You are _____

and _____ too!

Here is my Valentine's message for you:

_____

_____

FROM:

_____

How I Draw a Snowman

by _____

How do you draw a snowman? In the boxes, draw the steps to show how. Then write about the steps.

1. First, I _____

_____

2. Then, I _____

_____

3. Next, I _____

_____

4. Last, I _____

_____

Celebrate 100!

by _____

How did your class celebrate the 100th day of school? Draw a picture showing one way you celebrated.

In this picture, we are _____

_____

I liked this because _____

_____

We also celebrated by _____

_____

Some other ways we could celebrate are _____

_____

50 Month-by-Month Draw & Write Prompts Scholastic Professional Books

My Prediction

by _____

Do you think the groundhog will see its shadow this year? Draw a picture to show what you think will happen.

I think the groundhog _____

If the groundhog sees its shadow, _____

_____

If the groundhog does not see its shadow, _____

_____

I hope that _____

_____

Taking Care of My Teeth

by _____

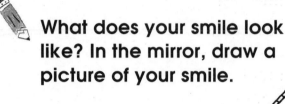

What does your smile look like? In the mirror, draw a picture of your smile.

Word Bank

- chew
- bite
- smile
- eat
- food
- munch
- crunch
- brush
- toothpaste
- dentist
- healthy

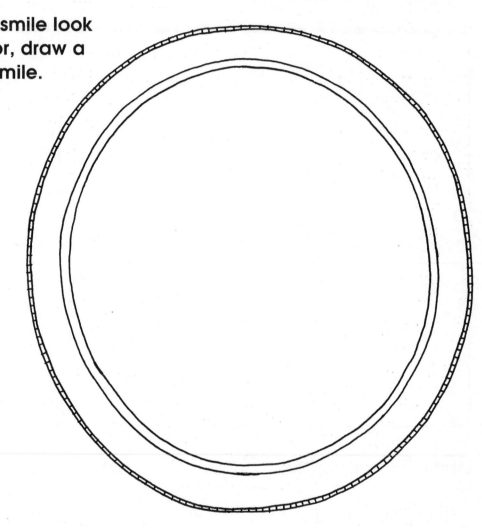

Teeth are important because _____

_____

I take care of my teeth by _____

_____

I have lost _____

On a Rainy Day

by _____

What do you like to do on a rainy day? Draw a picture to show what you like to do.

On a rainy day, I like to _____

_____

I like to do this because _____

_____

On a rainy day, I wear _____

On a rainy day, I feel _____

My Kite for Windy Weather

 Design your own kite!   **Then draw a picture of yourself flying your kite.**

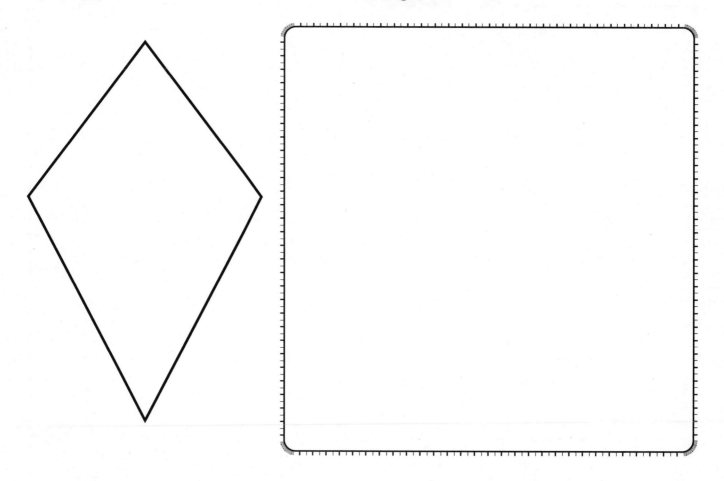

In this picture, I am _____

_____

A good place to fly a kite is _____

_____

I would like to fly a kite because _____

_____

50 Month-by-Month Draw & Write Prompts Scholastic Professional Books

Favorite School Activities

by _____

In each box, draw a picture of something you like to do at school. Write the name of the activity below each drawing. Then fill in the chart.

Draw your school activity picture here.	I like doing this because...	My favorite thing about this is...
Name of Activity _____		
Name of Activity _____		

My Wish on a Four-Leaf Clover

by _____

If you could make a wish on a four-leaf clover, what would you wish for? Draw a picture to show your wish.

If I found a four-leaf clover, I would wish for _____

_____

I would wish for this because _____

_____

If my wish came true, I would feel _____

If I found another four-leaf clover, I would wish for _____

_____

Eating Healthy Foods

by _____

 What kinds of healthy foods do you like to eat? Draw some of them on the plate below.

Some of the healthy foods I like to eat are _____

_____

I like these foods because _____

_____

It is good to eat these foods because _____

_____

April Fools!

by _____

Do you know a funny riddle or joke? Draw a picture to show your riddle or joke.

Write your joke here: _____

_____

_____

_____

Then share your joke or riddle with a classmate!

Signs of Spring

by _____

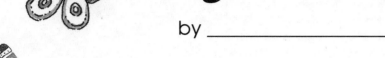

What things do you see when it is almost springtime? Draw a picture that shows some of the signs of spring.

When spring is almost here, I see _____

_____

I also see _____

The weather becomes _____

When it is springtime, I like to _____

_____

Taking Care of the Earth

by _____

 What can you do to take care of the Earth? In each box, draw something that you can do.

1.

In this picture, I am _____

_____

This helps the Earth because

_____

_____

2.

In this picture, I am _____

_____

This helps the Earth because

_____

_____

A Springtime Surprise!

by _____

**Use the key to color the shapes below.
You will find a springtime surprise!**

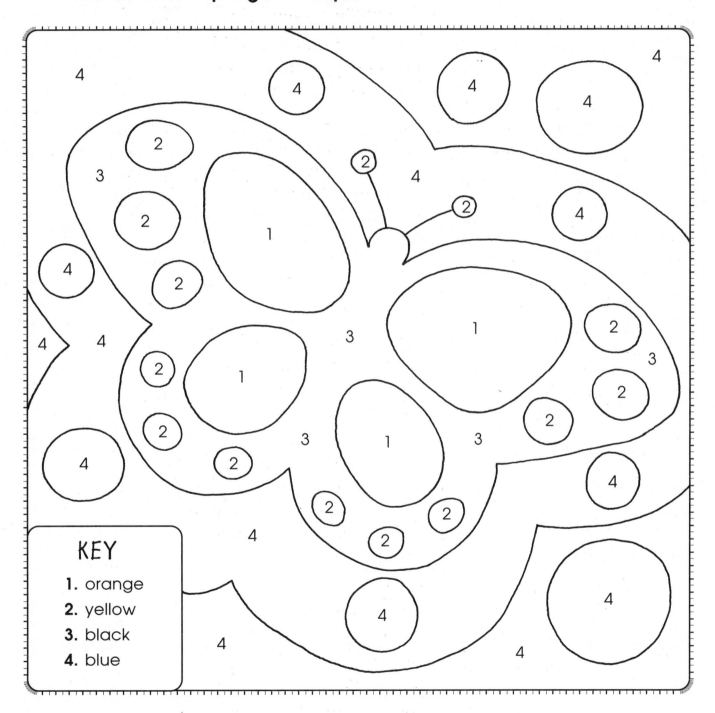

KEY

1. orange
2. yellow
3. black
4. blue

This is a picture of a _____

All About Butterflies

by _____

✏️ **In the box, draw a picture of a colorful butterfly.**

Word Bank
- fly
- flutter
- wings
- beautiful
- colorful
- caterpillar
- eat
- munch
- milkweed
- chrysalis
- springtime

Write three things you know about butterflies. Use the word bank if you need help.

1. _____

2. _____

3. _____

If I were a butterfly, I would _____

_____

My Favorite Bug

by _____

What is your favorite bug?
In the magnifying glass, draw a picture of it.

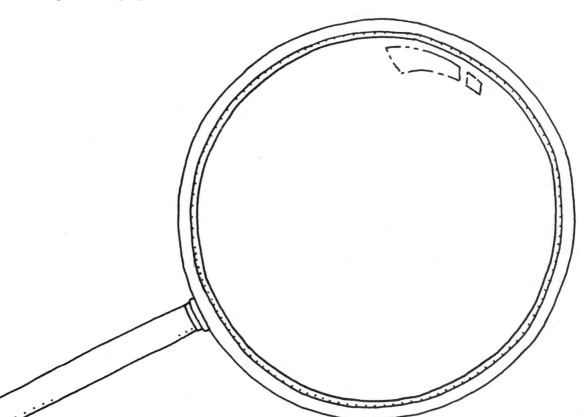

My favorite bug is _____

I like this bug because _____

_____

The following words describe this bug: _____

_____

If I could have this bug as a pet, I would name it _____

My Flower Journal

by _____

 Imagine that you are growing a flower. What would you say about it in your journal? Draw a picture of the flower's growth for each week. Start from when it was a seed.

Week 1

Today, I _____

_____

Week 2

This week _____

_____

Week 3

Now _____

_____

Week 4

Wow! _____

_____

50 Month-by-Month Draw & Write Prompts Scholastic Professional Books

Taking Care of Animals

by _____

Think of a pet that you have or would like to have. In the boxes, draw the steps to show how you would take care of your pet. Then write about the steps.

1. First, I _____
_____

2. Then, I _____
_____

3. Next, I _____
_____

4. Last, I _____
_____

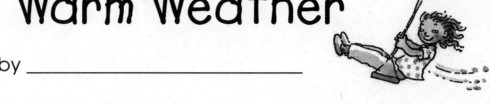

In Warm Weather

by _____

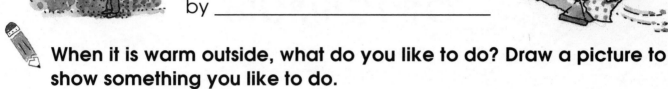

When it is warm outside, what do you like to do? Draw a picture to show something you like to do.

When it is warm outside, I like to _____

_____

I like doing this because _____

_____

When it is warm, I like to go to _____

_____

I like warm weather because _____

_____

50 Month-by-Month Draw & Write Prompts Scholastic Professional Books

My Own Flag

by _____

 Each country has its own flag. If you could have your own flag, what would it look like? Draw and color your flag below.

Word Bank

colorful

red

blue

yellow

green

pink

purple

stars

stripes

hearts

pictures

room

house

door

My flag is _____

_____

Something special about my flag is _____

_____

These are places I would hang my flag: _____

_____

Someone I Admire

by _____

Think of the people you learned about this year in school. Whom do you admire? In the frame, draw a picture of the person.

This is a picture of _____

This person is important because _____

_____

Something I admire about this person is _____

_____

50 Month-by-Month Draw & Write Prompts Scholastic Professional Books

What I've Learned...

by _____

Draw a picture to show something you learned this year.

[drawing box]

I learned how to _____

I learned this by _____

_____

Someone who helped me learn this was _____

I also learned to _____

Next year, I would like to learn _____

_____

Classmate Award

by _____

 Think about a classmate who can do something special. Draw a picture to show what he or she can do. Then fill in the award for your classmate.

Date _____

_____ deserves an award
(Name of Classmate)

because _____

_____.

Signed _____
(Your Name)

A Patriotic Surprise

by _____

**Use the key to color the shapes below.
You will find a patriotic surprise!**

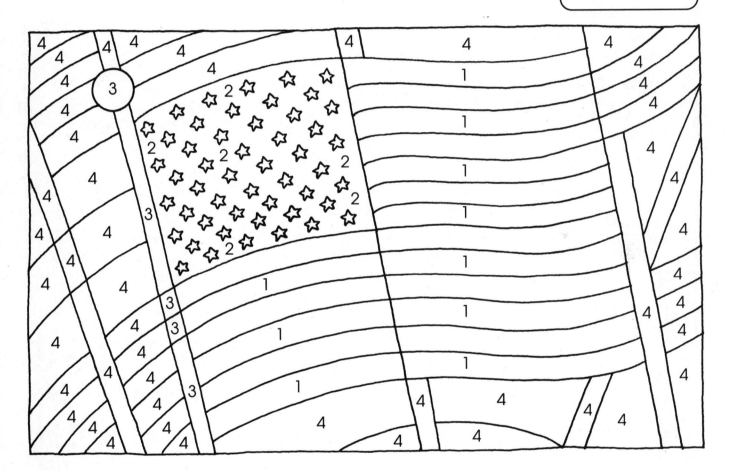

This is a picture of _____

All About Our Flag

by _____

Add stars and stripes to the flag below and color them in.

The colors of the American flag are _____

The American flag has _____

These are places where I see the American flag: _____

_____

People display the American flag because _____

_____

Celebrating Our Country

by _____

✏️ **Draw a picture of something you do to celebrate the Fourth of July.**

Word Bank

- eat
- play
- swim
- fireworks
- cookout
- picnic
- beach
- park
- country
- history
- family
- free
- proud
- happy

On the Fourth of July, I _____

_____

I celebrate this holiday with _____

_____

On the Fourth of July, I also like to _____

_____

We celebrate this holiday because _____

_____

Favorite Summertime Activities

by _____

In each box, draw a picture of something you like to do during the summer. Write the name of the activity below each drawing. Then fill in the chart.

Draw your summer activity picture here.	I like doing this because...	My favorite thing about this is...
Name of Activity		
Name of Activity		

Swim, Swim, Swim

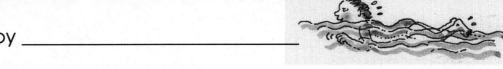

by _____

Draw a picture of yourself swimming.

I know how to _____

_____

I would like to learn how to _____

_____

I like to _____

_____

I like to go to the _____

Letter to a Friend

by _____

Imagine that you are going to write a letter to a friend.
Think of questions to ask in the letter.
Then think of something you would like to tell your friend.
In the box, draw a picture to show what you wrote about.

Date _____

Dear _____,

How _____?

What _____?

I hope that _____.

Something interesting that happened to me was

_____

_____.

Your friend,

_____

50 Month-by-Month Draw & Write Prompts Scholastic Professional Books